BOA
EDITIONS LTD

T0161146

FIELD NOTES FROM THE FLOOD ZONE

FIELD NOTES
FROM THE FLOOD ZONE

⋮

HEATHER SELLERS

American Poets Continuum Series, No. 192

BOA Editions, Ltd. • Rochester, NY • 2022

First Edition
22 23 24 25 7 6 5 4 3 2 1

For information about permission to reuse any material from this book, please contact The Permissions Company at www.permissionscompany.com or e-mail permdude@gmail.com.

Publications by BOA Editions, Ltd.—a not-for-profit corporation under section 501 (c) (3) of the United States Internal Revenue Code—are made possible with funds from a variety of sources, including public funds from the Literature Program of the National Endowment for the Arts; the New York State Council on the Arts, a state agency; and the County of Monroe, NY. Private funding sources include the Max and Marian Farash Charitable Foundation; the Mary S. Mulligan Charitable Trust; the Rochester Area Community Foundation; the Ames-Amzalak Memorial Trust in memory of Henry Ames, Semon Amzalak, and Dan Amzalak; the LGBT Fund of Greater Rochester; and contributions from many individuals nationwide. See Colophon on page 76 for special individual acknowledgments.

NATIONAL ENDOWMENT for the ARTS
arts.gov

State of the Arts
NYSCA

Cover Design: Sandy Knight
Cover Art: "Asleep, Adrift" by Judith Schaechter
Interior Design and Composition: Richard Foerster
BOA Logo: Mirko

BOA Editions books are available electronically through BookShare, an online distributor offering Large-Print, Braille, Multimedia Audio Book, and Dyslexic formats, as well as through e-readers that feature text to speech capabilities.

Library of Congress Cataloging-in-Publication Data

Names: Sellers, Heather, 1964- author.
Title: Field notes from the flood zone / Heather Sellers.
Description: First Edition. | Rochester, NY : BOA Editions, Ltd., 2022. |
    Series: American poets continuum series ; no. 192 | Summary: "Drawn from daily observations, Heather Sellers's poems ponder the changing Florida Coast as the population swells and the waters rise"— Provided by publisher.
Identifiers: LCCN 2021039142 (print) | LCCN 2021039143 (ebook) | ISBN 9781950774579 (paperback) |
    ISBN 9781950774586 (ebook)
Subjects: LCGFT: Poetry.
Classification: LCC PS3569.E5749 F54 2022 (print) | LCC PS3569.E5749 (ebook) |
    DDC 811/.54—dc23
LC record available at https://lccn.loc.gov/2021039142
LC ebook record available at https://lccn.loc.gov/2021039143

BOA Editions, Ltd.
250 North Goodman Street, Suite 306
Rochester, NY 14607
www.boaeditions.org
A. Poulin, Jr., Founder (1938–1996)

For John Brehm

Contents

— Part One —

— Part Two —

— Part Three —

— Part One —

Storm Season Opens

I placed quarter after quarter in the meter, seven minutes, seven minutes, same seven minutes, never receiving the two hours I'd already come to think of as mine.

I walked past the tourist shops, paintings of flowers and sharks. Pearl pendants, silver sand dollars and starfish. Waterfront real estate. Curry.

I touched unmated shoes on display and watched a long-haired dachshund refuse the cobbler's treat.

At a bar in this rain-steamed Southern city, I ordered salmon salad.

The woman next to me said to her friends, "I think there's a place in Orlando that is like an ice bar."

I take *like* as burnishing.

I read an essay on mystery, distinguishing what is secret from what is hidden.

As I took notes, the woman next to me said, "Let us know if you need any help."

"Are we okay here? Are we still okay?" the bartender said. She turned and I saw the back of her black silk blouse slit from nape to waist to show the words, an illegible cursive sentence tattooed down her spine.

After, I stepped out into the amphitheater of night to see jagged neon bolts stitching across the dome, the whole sky whitening, flash-flickering, the world about to go out, not wanting to go out.

The rains begin.

Virtual Life

At my kitchen counter, I enter an online classroom called Blackboard Ultra Hangout to speak with a student in pajamas about her novel-in-progress: too many characters, not enough trouble.

The termite inspector arrives. Have I seen any wings, frass? He climbs a ladder into my attic, two enormous flashlights hanging from his belt like swords, with a plastic clipboard, his small white shield.

When has a man last been inside my house?

At the corner store I purchase popcorn, wine, and a waxy yellow pepper, inexplicably stranded among inedibles.

Evening pours over the island.

I continue my quest to distinguish solitude, isolation, loneliness and aloneness.

The king tide rises obsidian.

I am on this small island in the Gulf, a bobber on a bobber.

And most nights I fall asleep as a child, the child who saved each blue bit of broken eggshell she found on sidewalks—for beauty, for muscle.

Mid-June, by Mid-Morning

The sky was greasy and gray, hard waves tipping over the seawall. I thought I had time to get to the bank—quick hop over the little white bridge.

Sheets of rain and slabs of water slide over the pavement, over the sidewalks. The intersection is already blocked by men in yellow slickers with hoods and bills. They wave with all their arms, *Turn back, turn back, turn back.*

When I pass the stone women on the boulevard, I pretend they are in conversation, not being spied on.

Sometimes the water comes up to our waists.

Rain

When it begins to rain, it rains every afternoon, or all day, and some nights are made more of water than darkness.

Raindrops the size of grapes, the shape of asteroids. There is sweet rain, greasy rain, new rain. Rain pools, settles in: the city is a glittering marsh.

I hold my palm out the window to weigh drops. They collected there, heavy as balls of mercury.

This kind, unnavigable, doesn't last long.

Through rain, I run from my house to my car in the driveway. My bare legs are cold-wet, my linen blouse spattered. All dry by the time I reach the grocery store.

When sweating after running in the rain, it's hard to tell what water's originally from where.

My hair rains its own kind of rain.

An umbrella provides a way to carry water inside with you, everywhere you go.

Late afternoon, I lie on my guest bed and make a video of rain pearls hanging onto the palm fronds slapping against the small window, as my friend did during a rare rain in winter, last December, when we lived in the previous world.

Cathedral

On Sunday I walked past the man stretched out on the granite steps and took a program from the usher at the great bronze doors.

Next to me in the pew a man in a fine suit kneeled and prayed, then, seated, he texted.

Jeremiah quoted God: *What does straw have in common with wheat*?

I fanned my face with the program and felt sweat run down my neck as the pastor spoke of disruption.

I did not kneel. I saw no children.

The dachshund in his roller bag eased up out of his compartment and whined, eyes closed, while we sang the doxology.

In the mosaic over the altar Jesus enters Jerusalem and I noticed the date palms around him were the same species as the ones lining the street outside the church, stout, holy, dinosaur-y.

When I walked back down the granite steps, I saw three empty cups and juice stains where the man had lain.

From the church parking lot, I watched lightning across the bay, bolts from volumizing thunderheads, on a sunny day, marching our way.

Saturday

I don't want to listen to the hard, high whines of leaf blowers' dissonant strains but I do so all morning, longing for the dusky hush of brooms.

I fight the troubled middle of my story.

I complain to my friend *I don't know.* But I do know.

For the party, I make deviled eggs and outfit each one with a cilantro leaf-sail stabbed into the yolk matter—twenty-four accented syllables.

Champagne: cold hard confetti liquefied in a sugary cage.

I drive home from the big house on high ground through rain, my car parting the beaded curtains of silver as though making way to a brand-new place.

Sinking

Men tear down the small house across the street and in trucks they carry the pieces away.

I watch the new hole there fill with rain.

All day the osprey pair fly in circles over their nest in the great white pine, then away.

The first hurricane of the season, spinning hard around its eye, heads towards our coast at a slow-walking pace: two miles per hour.

I drive to the beach, park my car on crushed shells. I sink into the shells.

Here even a small depression is significant.

I walk as though over broken glass into the wind. I want the wind to hold me up. I hold onto my hair.

In the chaos of waves, with wind from every direction, high cliffs of new dark sea fall and rise and drop over the beach.

People prepare for landfall but no one is prepared for landfall.

Here, in this place, summer is the long winter.

Flash Flood

I was making dinner, peeling radishes at the sink, when afternoon suddenly turned to pitch. Hail graveled against the windows.

From the porch, I watched sear-white rods fasten fire to the water. My spine bristled and I wondered if I'd been hit.

Evening cut loose as liquid. The strong sense of *sailing away*.

A gray sedan, stalled on my lawn, held a woman waving, window down, her voice sucked into the storm.

Do you want me to call someone? Lightning broke wild around my words and I felt like a powerful god speaking in pointless thunderbolts. She held her phone high, pointed to it.

Later, those two women, or two other women, waded into the remnants.

From this water come electric snakes, chemical blooms, the new world.

Later, inside, I lay in clear cool water in the old green bath as monks sang the Ordinary—struck by music's aqueous pauses and silvering—until we lost power.

Prone

I lit the lemon-scented candle on the windowsill.

I lay down on the floor.

I placed my mind in a brass bowl.

Then I misted the orchids.

I turned summary into scene.

I captured wool socks in a canvas pouch and zipped.

Late, I lay in my soft bed as a damp skeleton.

I dreamt of my mother: I was trying to fit my body through a tiny window in a door in order to escape her and join people listening to live music congregated behind a berm on the other side of the wall.

They could see my struggle but not understand it was real and I was alone.

Evacuation

I locked the front door and prayed my small house would live on its own.

I dragged my suitcase across the driveway turned to weeds. During storm season, every crevasse bursts with prehistoric fecundities.

"We live here because it's nice," the driver said, as we crossed the bridge to the airport by the bay. "Down at the beach, water comes to my door, but it's a nice area. Low crime."

From the plane, I saw the state of neat green squares, white scars, blue circles, highways coated with shining cars, the Florida coastline a hasty sketch line.

In New York the driver said, "You can sit in the front, ma'am, because the air is not going to get to the back of the cab."

Twin boys in matching camper shorts looked up at a tall sunflower not-yet-blossomed on the sidewalk on 34th Street as though it were the first one and the last one.

At the crosswalk, I stood behind a solid guy with an expensive haircut who said to his friend, "So what are we doing here? How does it relate to me?"

I walked through the steaming city holding its heat.

Museum (Zone A)

Color can be a formal problem and a political statement, I read on the mounted placard on the wall by the painting at the Whitney.

Andy Warhol's definition of Pop Art: *It's liking things*: Like how we like now on social media, says the curator, whom I do not like.

On this high floor, the painter states all of her paintings have as their subject: home, safety, endurance, intensity.

Below, the Hudson River, ribbons of sea stream past, sculpting the piers, etching the banks, visibly rising.

In the elevator much larger than my bathroom at home, I descend to the plaza level where I walk along the base of the museum.

Naval designers, builders of submarines, redrew all of the plans after Hurricane Sandy, when the site filled with deep black water and water spilled over little buildings, out the windows and into the nights. Now great floodgates, Knox-thick, three stories high, hide in the wings, so exquisitely balanced a person can push them closed with one hand.

"We think of the art as being patients," the architect says to the reporter. "We don't want them to die."

Threat

The eye wall solidifies in the Gulf and in the city so do I.

At the Amazon store in Columbus Circle, a new section is titled "Books People Read in Three Days on Kindle."

The breeze in New York is southerly, humid, all Florida in my flimsy skirt.

Forecaster Forester posts their report at 11 a.m., in thick Courier: All interests in Florida should have completed final preparations.

Every storm has a childhood.

I don't want to grow accustomed.

A man in a tuxedo asks as I pass the original basilica on Prince, *Are you looking for the Catacombs tour?*

Not today.

North Coast

The goshawk flew low from the pines into the deepest wood. As though right out of my head.

One thousand miles from home, I walked across the high dune, past Victorian fish scale houses and elegant new homes, down to the great lake roaring far below.

Up and down the coastline, broken and dangling wooden stairs hung off the face of the sheared away, fallen-in dune.

Riprap and revetments poked out from dune grass, frizzled lines among old surfboards and timber—attempts. Strands of fencing and bright torn lawn chairs stabbed into the sand like flags, as if to bury themselves, and the navy-blue waves of water came up over it all, crashing *hush, away, hush.*

Further down the ridge, men with flatbed trucks slid an old house off its pilings, moving it back from the edge.

I walked back up the narrow lane, Joy Road, past spent milkweed and chalky fleabane, past gargantuan decorative pumpkins. A woman with a spaniel on a leash said as she passed, "Isn't it a beautiful day?"

After the Storm

From the airport, I ride in Bat's Taxi out to New Tampa, high ground an hour inland to retrieve my car from my ex's garage.

I let myself into his house with the key he has me keep.

In his tiled dining room, I study the painting he made of his dog. I love as I have always loved the carrot floating over the dog's head, shining.

I drive around the manicured neighborhood, Tampa Palms, in effusive air conditioning. It is so good to be cold.

I pick him up from the university. We gobble red curry on rice, strange good mush. We speak as lovers and as former lovers, kind and concerned, laughing, close and far apart, some unwieldy wanting knocking around.

The evening sky is smooth silver, like a shell. I drive across the causeway toward home. The water is easy in the bay, light ink.

I see many tire marks along the sidewalls of the bridge. I make my way to the coast alone.

Home

The highway empty, the Holiday Motel shuttered.

Traffic lights dark, eyes closed. The angry pulse of adult drivers taking turns at intersections, stranded on their frazzled honor.

We are open! Avocado, tomato, bread, wine, pecans, rice.

The streets are full of standing gray water, a city of wide canals.

A wet rat walks along the top of the battered trellis with a cigarette.

I unlock the door and heat rushes out.

As in a fairy tale, I do not want to enter. For a second, I sense my mother, emerging from shadow.

This was before I knew about the black snake in the living room, rising, uncoiling, a leather tube of silent tune.

Protection

I woke with a dream of many flamingos flying low, landing en masse, all walking now gently toward my body.

I went to Publix for noodles and Dawn.

I stopped at Fatima's Alterations to pick up the tunic whose sleeve I'd torn raising my arm too quickly and urgently in the city.

A young schefflera—umbrella tree—sprang from the roof as though my house had a bright idea.

I watched the black felt sky lose its softness as evening and storm came together quickly, outlining my loneliness.

That's when I noticed the caladiums I planted before the storm, slender black fingernails pierced from the dirt and shining in the rain, curling *come, this way, this way.*

High Tide

A great white heron flies low over a street filled with ink-dark water. The utility truck breaks the water into waves and whitecaps, and the image of the bird dissolves into the ruffled edge of the water as though the bird and foam are made from the same liquid chemical white matter.

When the water recedes: cushion, two-by-four, recycling bin, shrub, rushes of leathery fronds, a van. A sedan stranded on the neighbor's lawn. Moccasins.

Mold blooms on the lawns, thick blue coatings in ragged continents, as though hastily spray-painted for a coming event.

Between Storms

I pull weeds from the driveway, and heat from white roots spirals up the veins in my arms.

A whistling man rides past on a foldable bicycle. He does not seem to see me kneeling by the low hedge, thus I experience myself as an animal.

While I am making dinner, a letter from my mother, 2004, drops out of a book of recipes. *I wish you could forgive the terrible events of the past. You used to be a good person!* And a drawing, by her signature, of a single heavy teardrop.

I fold and stack soft clothes, still warm from the dryer. I hold them to my chest. I do not put them away because the path is not yet clear— evacuation suitcase? Dresser drawers? When? To where? To whom?

A Cut

I see her mail truck idling down on Rafael, in the center of the street where grass grows from standing water

Sometimes I see her waving from over on Cordova, wading to houses where the sausage trees stand in salt water, sausage-ing.

The news reports as "very rare events" the flesh-eating bacteria that killed a man in Sarasota who dove here in the river. And the flesh-eating bacteria killed the boy from Ohio who swam here in the emerald sea.

The reporter says, *Don't swim if you have an open cut.* And he mentions depth and nostrils.

Pool

Two sedans spun in slow motion before me in the intersection, metal sliding through draperies of rain. I held onto my neck with both hands.

For hours in a windowless room, I spliced digital video and created many fades, just so. But I could not save my projects in the media bin. I did not know I could only save things if at the very outset I named them.

I drove through showers, threading along flooded streets to my friend with the salt-water swimming pool. Her front door was half open and gold light poured out as a dry path to her home.

When I entered the foyer, I noticed her husband standing on the stairs. I bowed into his glowering.

In her pool we swam sidestroke in the rain, facing each other, talking while I looked for lightning. The sky was gray and low, thick on us, and I did not know for certain what I saw, just that we had to get out.

But as we climbed out, we noticed squirming: baby snapping turtles stranded in the filter basket.

Treading, she pulled them out one by one. I set the mottled carapaces down by the retention pond in the marshy grasses. Tilted there and closed, the awful fists stilled.

Longing, Wading

Marble statues from the 1920s line our island's promenade. The women have lost their arms and what they were holding. Boys are losing their faces.

They would not be turning and bending if there was no narrative.

Key elements of the hunt, heartbreak—a quiver, an empty vase—remain.

I tried to explain to my friend the concept of neglect for orchids.

To Kyle P. from Florida Pest Control, who picked up by its tail the dead bug on my living room floor with his bare thumb and forefinger—*This, ma'am is your American cockroach*—I said, *Thank you.* But I meant *How?*

Today's rain is not the kind that gets you wet. More of a blossoming.

Careful, Unfurling

There were pauses, risks to take, temporary escapes.

The golf course tested the emergency alert system, an air raid siren, this morning, first Friday of the month.

The system was working.

My editor listed what she liked, what she didn't understand, what made her cry at her desk, and I took notes.

The neighbor's pool overflowed all storm season long, sliding down my driveway on its whitening way to the bay.

The osprey returned to the abandoned pine. She screamed from the tattered old nest.

She screamed all day over the water.

"You don't have to come to me," I told my friend. "I'll come to you. I want to see you. I will bring caladiums."

And the lizards leapt from the pentas onto the ground, the dun mourning doves perched perfectly still on the electrical wires, and a plane flew overhead, to the north, disappearing into a pale blue sky as though *the end*.

But Why Do We Live Here?

Ellen: Because it's *paradise*. Look around!

Me: Don't you worry?

Ellen: I don't. Maybe I should? But I don't. Honey, it's *February*. Enjoy life!

— Part Two —

Fun for Everyone Involved

As a girl, I lived with my father in a pink duplex on the west side of Orlando. I slept in a brown velour recliner on a jalousie-windowed porch. My father, Fred, slept in a king-size bed that filled the bedroom, and I never went in that room, it was all mattress.

We lived on a dirt road, McCleod. Interstate Highway 4 ran along the dirt road, and there was always a cloud of dust over the hot lawn. The drainage ditch got fenced in over Christmas, and come spring, an alligator rose up, out of the emerald green muck, inside the fence. My father and I named him Li'l Fella. Come summer, we renamed him Big Fella.

I saw my father feed him old chicken. Saw him throw bread over the fence around the ditch. A kettle of scorched soup.

The gator lived in a cage, in essence. We named him to love him, but it did not feel right to know him this way. My father standing at the chain link, a tumbler of gin in one hand, his face already off-sides, early afternoon. Banging on the fence, hollering, *Want some what, Big Fella? What do you want?*

I thought maybe we had it all wrong. And not just the story we told ourselves about Big Fella. *All of it.*

For example, that gator could be a girl. Could have no name.

My father said we'd grill him, Fourth of July. He said that just to rile me, and it did rile me.

My father said I could not ever move out.

I slept in a brown velour chair that tilted back. Not a bed. I had to move out.

Boys who lived one trailer over told me Desmond threw a dog inside that fence. It was true I could see blood, black now, on the wire.

It was awesome.

Throw you in there, my father loved to say. *Can you swim? How fast?* Every time he said *fast,* he reached down and grabbed one of my thighs with both his ice-wet hands, and leaned over, bit my shoulder.

Chomp, he liked to say. *Chomp.*

Oh come on. Don't be that way. We're just having fun.

My Mother Said

Never touch your body. Never touch anyone's body. Never let anyone touch your body.

Where did you hear that? No. We don't need to be getting into all of that. Where did you hear that?

Why are you walking like that? It's like you are sticking out your bottom on purpose.

Can you please put some more clothes on?

Your body is sacred. Your body is your *temple*.

What do you mean, what does that mean?

You have cramps because you eat too fast. You don't chew.

There's no reason for you to shave your legs. Why would you even want to do that?

You're trying to attract attention—the wrong kind of attention.

Please don't sit like that.

Are you trying to wear makeup? Wouldn't it be better if you just brushed your hair?

You've gained weight, honey. Can you not see it? You've gotten so heavy, so fast. What are you eating?

Take care of your body, take care of your body, take care of your body.

Oh, you're so smart, so wise. I know. You're in college. You know *everything*. But you are going to get diseases. You could get cancer, behaving as you do. Cancer. Do yourself a favor: Read up.

Cover up. For crying out loud, please cover up your body. I can see everything. People can see everything—you can't see it.

Can you get your hair cut shorter, honey? It might be more flattering to your face.

You need a slip.

You need a bra.

You need pantyhose.

You should be wearing support pantyhose. Where is the support hose I sent you? You're going to get veins; they run in our family.

You get too much sun.

You can't wear that in public. Why don't you pull yourself together and look as nice as I know you can?

Brush!

Those girls, painted up like that. Spending all that precious time and money on their clothes and hair. Staring at themselves in the mirror: *Oh, look at me, look at me.*

Women who dye their hair—who do they think they're fooling?

You can't come in my house looking like that.

You can't leave my house looking like that.

If you have this skirt taken in, are you absolutely sure you aren't going to gain the weight back? Are you going to be able to discipline yourself, stick to a diet? Are you exercising? Is this alteration worthwhile?

Your father is not an athletic person, but he's a brilliant man.

You have nice arms, honey. I would say your best feature.

We *all* wish we had more of a chin.

You are a beautiful swimmer. I will contribute half to a pool membership if you will sign a statement that you'll go swimming three times a week.

I will pay to have your teeth fixed. I'll pay if you think you can find a good dentist. I'll send the money directly to him.

The overdevelopment in Florida—it's criminal. The way they let people just keep pouring in.

But you know what I'm really worried about? These storms.

My Father Said

Come here. Come closer. Come on. Don't be like that. Come see your ole daddy.

Put your finger in my mouth. I don't bite.

Oh, come on now. That didn't hurt; that was a love bite. You're not hurt. You're fine.

That couldn't possibly have hurt; it was a love tap.

I didn't mean that one to be so hard.

Stop being that way. Come on now.

You're my daughter. My girl chile. I can too do that.

I'm a befuddled person. Maybe you have some insight? Why do so many people do the opposite of what is clearly in their own best interest? Maybe you can explain it to me?

You're getting broad in the beam.

Let me feel you.

Come here. I can't reach you.

When you coming back home? When you coming home?

It was raining in the living room, raining inside for a long while.

I need you to come home to fill out these forms, all this paperwork. Yes, we got damage. We got hit.

There's a tree in the garage and the roof is messed up bad.

I've got to get some help getting this carpet out.

Has anyone heard from your mother?

I lost all my rose bushes and all my meat.

Come on home, now. Help your ole daddy now.

I need help. I need to get reimbursed. Fill out these forms now for me, girl chile. C'mon.

— Part Three —

Thunderbird Motel

Heide drives over from Jungle Prada in her mom's old gold-plated-trim Lincoln and I fall into its caramel depths as a patient.

We glide out Central Avenue, the road to the beach, as winter goddesses.

We park for free in a hidden alley, trespass over narrow sand paths between the pastel cottages held together with staples and glue and hope and tarpaper, all yesteryear & low expectations.

A year after the storm, we still see its signature in blue roof tarps and new windows.

Because of our fathers, we share a strong sense of where damage hides and why.

This island, Treasure Island, is a sand bar with a six-lane road streaming with cars. It's hard to cross over from our side to the beach.

A Midwestern woman (gauze gauchos, blue-gold permanent puff of hair) carries cylinders of beer in her bike basket.

My childhood afternoons mound here, in hidden corners, interior corridors. I don't want to cross over.

Weekends at the coast with my father live as mysteries in my body, and I'm queasy, as I follow my friend, single file, to the sea.

Motel window unit air conditioners flicker, dented silver boxes, rattling, dripping hard drops. We walk under them, through the breezeway—as sketches, former girls.

"Sanding Ovations," massive sculptures of sand, line the beach in front of the grand hotel ready for judging.

Is that a globe with a mask of a woman's face? A brain of sand or two women kissing?

Various sized pairs of praying hands in an assemblage. Two gigantic humanoid skeletons, half-buried in the sand, embracing with their sand bone arms.

A strong feeling of not understanding the passions that move the makers, the crowd lined along the ropes.

We walked to the water's edge to watch the sun set: two women, frozen on the shore, ancient in our winter griefs.

The green flash!

Heide took a photo of us, just after the sun set. We appear grainy and overly still.

Florida

Johnny came down from Michigan and caught a little lemon shark, then a stingray. Maybe the wingspan was four feet—it was hard to tell with all the flying around.

The ray fought like a rattlesnake and bent around like a cat—his description. Which I liked so much I wrote it down. The strangeness of energy in our boat, the unholy action of trying to land a beast that does not belong to us.

I caught a puffer fish, tennis-ball-yellow, spined, see-through. Pulling the hook from her cheek was like taking a pin from paper. Gold light came through her strange stretched-thin skin. She was transparent when I lobbed her back, globe & window into the unseeable galaxy of sea.

Boats decorated with Christmas lights and stuffed elves in striped stockings tied to their masts passed us, too fast, racing to some blessing on the horizon.

We walked back to my house, a long, long way. Towards the end, I felt like a fish with feet.

Golf carts blinked bright strands of lights, wreaths on the front, grandchildren hanging off the back, thrilled and mute and bored, and tinny music, the kind called "festive," all the major keys.

"We're the Tipsy Elves," women called from a red golf cart, proffering from their palms vials of liquor, small bottles of wine.

As I stepped across my lawn, the sprinklers burst on in great fans, dry season wet.

The deep green St. Augustine grass sparkled with droplets of water in the late light and the sky turned hot pink and red.

We live in stolen jewelry.

The First Time I Went to His House

We sat on the sofa in the Japanese room. "I cleaned," he said. The lamps glowed. The tile floor shone.

We spoke softly for a long time. I knew he missed his wife but not how.

He kissed me on the forehead. He put his lips to my lips. Now his grief was my grief, too.

The dog padded over, all tail and tea table, offering wanting.

I lay my head in his lap and petted the dog.

We walked her down the street in the warm afternoon, gray light, late fall in Florida, no rain for months.

He whispered as we passed the houses. Ovarian cancer. Prostate cancer. A low tan house: cancer of the tongue. *Those two just moved in together. They lost their spouses, met in grief group, and now her cancer is back.*

Let's turn here, I said. I could tell he didn't really want to deviate from the regular loop. But the dog was pulling *Yes yes yes.*

I was her dream.

Let's just see what's over there, I said. Cypress trees, the black mirror of shallow water, a tupelo, sweet gum.

It wasn't really a street. A stub. Part of the subdivision that didn't divide right, a remainder.

I saw through the forest a strand of great new houses, mansions.

The dog nuzzled in her heaven.

We didn't speak. We did not speak one word. And I drove home late alone.

*

Now, the night is so black in winter.

The mansions sink into the softness of the swamp.

Between us is the cold sea, the heart-shaped bay.

The last time I went to his house was for shelter from the storm.

Dinner on the Patio, December

Leaves from the banyan dropped down onto the trays I'd prepared with olives, artichokes, figs.

The great cardboard leaves rang on the patio like soft bells.

The friends visiting from Michigan said, *So beautiful, so beautiful.* Their years-before tiny gift pot of rosemary was now a small tree.

I told them I was moving to higher ground. No, they said. *It's too beautiful here and so well-cared for.*

I imagined us speaking in bubbles, our coral chairs on the bottom of the sea.

But not for years, they said. *Can't you stay one more year?*

As they left, they hugged me tight, as though I am at risk of being washed away into the night.

And every night I am washed away by night.

After the Gala

He waited at his car in my drive until I was in. *I'm in*, I said to the night. I flashed my porch light. He nodded, then sailed away slowly in his black sedan, a creature.

I spun in my foyer in the dark.

My dress swirled like a ribbon.

The wine had come in courses, waves. Five, six glasses at every place. My strategy? Never finish anything.

Now, I drew a glass of cool water from the tap and drank.

I watched the moon through my kitchen window. My dress subsided. My sandals grew sleepy. How empty my house, my pretty pink house. I felt like a bee inside a flower past midnight.

What am I doing here?

I patted my hair, encapsulated in tight twists, and shellacked, looped coils, a phantasmagoric up-do to undo.

Could I sleep on this head? Sleep on a reef of coral.

I pulled out the pins, one by one, to count them. Ninety-three black bobby pins.

I, alone in the dark at fifty-one, partway undone.

Aftermaths

I returned my stepson back to the small airport by the sea.

How do you always know where you are going? he asked. He meant how was I not using my phone.

I told him how afraid I was here and of searching for work in a safer place, like where we used to live, up north, no storms.

But the university is on the water, he said. *The hospital. The air force base. It seems really nice here.*

That evening on a patio downtown, I sat with two poets, speaking of lines, sons, mothers, all the other kinds of weather.

While we talked, across Beach Drive in the park, professionals hung a great parti-colored net—art, precious and fine—from stanchions down by the bay.

This was the first day after the last day of storm season.

Category Five

When I drive up the old coast road along the Gulf, I see closed motels with empty postage stamp pools out front, fenced with chain link.

Bare flea markets, stump sellers, and many purveyors of life-sized fiberglass novelty sharks, manatees and mermaids, hanging from oak trees, mounted on flat roofs, faded in the sun.

I sense the ghost of my father in the empty fields here, pass the wasteland remnants of the trailer park where we lived. A pile of shag carpet, acrid mildew, beer cans, middens of the impoverished alcoholic life.

At the edge of my childhood, the state forest.

And on the outskirts of Blountstown—I'm sixty miles and an hour, more, from the coast—all the trees are broken. In every direction, forever to the horizon, there are no trees, just pale, broken posts.

Young green trees are broken and bent all in one direction, northeast.

It looks as though there's a hard wind blowing from the sea, bending every tree, but it's January. The actual air is motionless, overcast and plain.

The broken trees are stripped of their leaves and bark.

Homes are piles of lumber and junk. Dead trees are stacked along the highway, still, a year after the storm.

As I drive, for an hour, I see the fingerprint of the hurricane, the rotation, the young trees are blown north, then northwest, then southwestward.

In every direction to the horizon, the pale posts shimmer in silence over the bare land.

Still Life, Blountstown Gas Station

Me: All these trees, all from Michael?

Cashier: Oh it goes all the way up into Georgia like that. Way up. Way, way up. This is just some.

Me: Have you been down to the coast?

Cashier: I can only go as far as Panama City. That's as close as I've been able to handle. I can't go to Mexico Beach.

Me: I can't imagine how terrifying it must have been.

Cashier: And a lot of people are from somewhere else, so they don't know. I didn't know. I didn't even know really how bad a 2 is. And we had a 5.

          We stayed. Our house was destroyed around us. Next time, we'll leave. We didn't know.

          We found people before they found people.

Me: Terrifying.

Cashier: Pretty terrifying.

Transubstantiation at the Aquatic Life Research Center

Are you open? I called to the young man hunched over an empty blue concrete pit in the Quonset hut on the small barrier island.

Everything died, he said, not looking up.

I stepped inside. There was a low table with crayons, tiny chairs, and a box of broken shells. Aquariums on tables. On the ceiling, water light.

They turned off the pressure last night. They didn't tell me. There's no communication.

In a large tank in the center of the hot room, I bent to see giant scallops, their rims of eyes black, not blue. Ribbons of translucent white flesh, shirred, wavered in the still water.

He put his face down into his hands. He said, *It all could have been saved.*

A small green sea turtle floated on its side against the glass, and a vacant sea horse hovered as a clef.

I did not know what was dead or what was possible. I watched the sea creatures, as though watching closely could bring back life.

Come quick, said the young man from across the room. *A caterpillar, going into chrysalis!*

At the dry aquarium, I stood so close to him I felt his heat. We leaned over in tandem.

The black and white and yellow striped caterpillar hung from the branch. It curled into a tighter and tighter *J* and then a spiral.

Bright green skin slipped along the bottom, then the sides, then the green pouch zipped itself at the top.

The stem from which it hung grew thicker, blacker.

The emerald earring swayed gently in the glass box.

I said, *I've seen one coming out of chrysalis, but never going in.*

Why I had to speak aloud, I am not certain. I wanted to be *with*.

The next phase: the liquid mystery.

I guess now we're really closed, he said.

The tightness in my back, that raw knot between my wing blades from bending and hoping for so long, so hard, faded after about three days.

Dry Season

Jasmine strangles its own string bean fruit turned to black streaks on the trellis.

The banyan drops fleshy yellow leaves hourly coating the back patio with living curling.

Sausage trees over on Cordova Avenue silently chime, the long, long brown pods hanging, swinging.

Winter water in late afternoon is a mirror, a mirror for self, city, sun.

At the coast, I startle a flock of black skate flying through a shallow sky of water.

At sunset, a bride drags her train across the sand as she walks alone to the gathering, carrying a bouquet of white flowers from far away, some manufactured spring. Ranunculus, I think.

The clock on the pink hotel says 6:20, but it's not.

Jellyfish are stranded on the sand, pink, like raw chicken breasts and every few feet I step around one carefully.

For a long moment I stand ankle deep in ice cold water to stare at thonged women's bare bottoms, browning on striped towels in the winter sun.

Hollow spiny urchins, pallid gray, spiked with former world magnificence even in death. And the urge to pick one up, touch tongue to needle tip is strong, like craving a drink. To pierce!

Thus I wade away from the wedding gathering, away from the small tinny speakers playing *Once, twice, three times a lady,* which seems an impossible number of times to be a lady, and I'm moving in slow motion into the evening of my life yearning to know everything I see before me.

Translation

The poison potato tree limbs each hang heavy with massive squashes strung from long lengths of thin frazzled twine.

I worry about our heads and leaching.

In the sun, I lay on my patio and read Epictetus though I do not trust his buoyant translator from 1912.

The real estate agent Nancy Boissant arrives at six p.m., in darkness, in her black Lexus on the solstice.

Have to pressure wash. Call my Soft Wash guy. Costs a couple thou but so worth.

Is the Property located in a Special Hazard Zone?

The property is located on Earth.

Drown

The guava tree hides its hard, green fruits now—though no one eats them, not even the rats.

The grand old mango leans so hard to the south—trying to escape late life ankle-deep in salt water, storm-worn.

Black mildew coats the clay barrel tiles on my roof and every leaf on the potted lemon tree.

Lacy trees sprout from the gutters. It's like hair springing from the ears of a lover.

At night in my bed, almost every night, I dream I'm underwater.

Sometimes I breathe underwater. Sometimes I drown face down.

My Viper

Snarl on the tile, branch-black gecko horned and hooded, dropped to the floor, he rushes me, the footed snakelet, my dark king of the laundry room, his tiled empire. He rears up and in the frazzle I see his great green heart, the pulse of purple blood, too, and the teeth.

His bite is ragged, ready. Just like mine. We both have scars.

I can't kill a creature with a fine bone skeleton, ancient dreams, *teeth*.

Sometimes, I try to lure him towards a much better life, relocation, hints of Eden, with green leaves in a box, a bottle cap of cool water.

Thus we share our unhappiness, stalking, and despair of laundry.

We are wed: a reptile the size of an index finger, a woman the size of her scream.

Vortex

The intracoastal river along Florida's coast is a deep blue crease between the mainland and the barrier islands—hyphens and dashes—
that fills every day sideways with tides.

At island tips the river water meets its sea and spirals churn.

The new high tide flows sea over river water and the last low tide pulls out old river underneath—many layers of chaos.

People love points, the ends of places. Many wade in here, dive and drown, along with the people who jump in after to save them, friends, lovers, strangers.

Today I kneel on the beach and watch the water slice and churn. This kind of watching adds a layer of prayer.

When I was young, I waded in just here. I dove through the switchbacks of water, between rays of light and fish, into the storm under the surface.

The whirling water matched the vortex inside of me and the thrilling feeling didn't seem like fear. Back then it felt like healing.

I loved feeling lost and spun in dark roiling water, how it held me in silence within silence.

Florida Gold

In December, on the promenade along Coffee Pot Bayou, the mullet men cast their nets. They empty the catch on the sidewalk and squeeze the fish by the necks. White mucous comes from the mouth, female—her roe is $1.25 per pound. No mucous, male; sperm roe is 10 cents per pound.

The fish flick the sidewalk, beat it red with blood.

Golf carts, winterized with plastic wrapping, stay on the streets for roe season.

Every afternoon, a man in a wicker basket floats low in the heavy sky over the bay, hung from a great yellow sail, waving, as though flapping one wing.

I paddle along, wishing the fish clear of the nets, and the mullet men their dough.

And every day the manatee, her eyes warm as dogs' eyes, her back scarred with propeller white lashes, marine kanji, glides alongside.

Always her little one tucked next to her tail, sea cow apostrophe.

It's against the law for me to touch her but she is allowed to touch me and once she placed her flipper on my board.

We were so light on the water that day, floating softly as a pod of three, moving silently away from the men, away and into the great mouth of the open bay.

From Florida

The sea was the sea then and the bay was a little dish—you could see the bright white sand through clear water—and the small white bridge to Coffee Pot Riviera, built in 1924, shone high above the water, an arch over the sweet shallow blue of the bayou.

Our parents lived here, with Meyer lemon trees in the side yard and a world of familiar bugs.

Then the coyotes came to the golf course and took many small dogs and house cats—carried them away in their mouths like fur purses.

New bugs came in great hordes from all over the globe and the storms arrived in July and stayed through November.

Yesterday, I walked downtown, past the tourist shops, broken parking meters.

There was a strange cold rain in February. I passed a girl in a parka.

A brand-new life-size hammerhead shark made of poker chips swam from the ceiling in a glassy gallery, swaying with his grin.

The woman behind the counter called me to come in and see him, really see him. "Isn't he great? We call him 'Lucky'."

Coming Soon! New Home + Pool & Spa

At the home across the street, my house's twin, the foundation cracked and the slab broke open.

Mold slithered into every crevasse and the world there came to smell of fresh ammonia and loss.

Excavators broke the abandoned building into bite-size pieces of wall, appliance, cupboard and door shard and timber and the next day the land was razed of its oaks. Creatures' homes and wings and eggs and busted wiry matter were mixed together, trundled away in trucks.

The equinoctial storms swept away the lemon trees, the mango along the fence and the fence. The lot lay bare for years.

I watched the sunset from my front stoop, sky fire, then the elliptical line of the planets. Every night, the mechanics of poetry.

Early this morning, dawn, men arrived in flatbed trucks stacked with blocks, a cement truck. With gray slurry and concrete, they built a great gray box ten feet high off the ground.

Trucks returned to fill the container with white sand and dark dry dirt in layers.

Now there's a full-color image of the house that will sit on top, a modern mansion. A pretend slender white mother and father and girl, holding hands, walk up to their dream house built in the future sea.

Acknowledgments

The Adroit Journal: "Protection";

Birmingham Poetry Review: "Longing, Wading," "Florida Gold";

Blackbird: "Dinner on the Patio, December," "Aftermaths," "Category Five," "Transubstantiation at the Aquatic Life Research Center";

Body: "Pool";

Brevity: "Fun for Everyone Involved";

The Cincinnati Review: "Florida";

New Letters: "Sinking," "Prone," "Evacuation," "Museum (Zone A)," "Threat," "North Coast," "Home," "High Tide," "A Cut," "Careful, Unfurling," "But Why Do We Live Here?";

On the Seawall: "Flash Flood," "Between Storms";

Prism: "Storm Season Opens," "Mid-June, by Mid-Morning," "Rain";

The Sun: "My Mother Said," "My Father Said."

About the Author

A Florida native, Heather Sellers teaches in the creative writing program at the University of South Florida. She is the author of a popular textbook, *The Practice of Creative Writing,* and three previous collections of poetry: *Drinking Girls and Their Dresses, The Boys I Borrow*, and *The Present State of the Garden.* Her essays appear in *The New York Times, Best American Essays*, and *The Pushcart Prize: Best of the Small Presses.* She has also published a children's book, *Spike and Cubby's Ice Cream Island Adventure,* and a book of Florida-based short stories, *Georgia Underwater,* and she is the recipient of fellowships from the NEA and MacDowell. Her memoir, *You Don't Look Like Anyone I Know,* tells the story of coming to terms with prosopagnosia (face blindness). Her website is heathersellers.com.

BOA Editions, Ltd.
American Poets Continuum Series

No. 1 *The Fuhrer Bunker: A Cycle of Poems in Progress*
W. D. Snodgrass

No. 2 *She*
M. L. Rosenthal

No. 3 *Living With Distance*
Ralph J. Mills, Jr.

No. 4 *Not Just Any Death*
Michael Waters

No. 5 *That Was Then: New and Selected Poems*
Isabella Gardner

No. 6 *Things That Happen Where There Aren't Any People*
William Stafford

No. 7 *The Bridge of Change: Poems 1974–1980*
John Logan

No. 8 *Signatures*
Joseph Stroud

No. 9 *People Live Here: Selected Poems 1949–1983*
Louis Simpson

No. 10 *Yin*
Carolyn Kizer

No. 11 *Duhamel: Ideas of Order in Little Canada*
Bill Tremblay

No. 12 *Seeing It Was So*
Anthony Piccione

No. 13 *Hyam Plutzik: The Collected Poems*

No. 14 *Good Woman: Poems and a Memoir 1969–1980*
Lucille Clifton

No. 15 *Next: New Poems*
Lucille Clifton

No. 16 *Roxa: Voices of the Culver Family*
William B. Patrick

No. 17 *John Logan: The Collected Poems*

No. 18 *Isabella Gardner: The Collected Poems*

No. 19 *The Sunken Lightship*
Peter Makuck

No. 20 *The City in Which I Love You*
Li-Young Lee

No. 21 *Quilting: Poems 1987–1990*
Lucille Clifton

No. 22 *John Logan: The Collected Fiction*

No. 23 *Shenandoah and Other Verse Plays*
Delmore Schwartz

No. 24 *Nobody Lives on Arthur Godfrey Boulevard*
Gerald Costanzo

No. 25 *The Book of Names: New and Selected Poems*
Barton Sutter

No. 26 *Each in His Season*
W. D. Snodgrass

No. 27 *Wordworks: Poems Selected and New*
Richard Kostelanetz

No. 28 *What We Carry*
Dorianne Laux

No. 29 *Red Suitcase*
Naomi Shihab Nye

No. 30 *Song*
Brigit Pegeen Kelly

No. 31 *The Fuehrer Bunker: The Complete Cycle*
W. D. Snodgrass

No. 32 *For the Kingdom*
Anthony Piccione

No. 33 *The Quicken Tree*
Bill Knott

No. 181 *Caw*
Michael Waters

No. 182 *Letters to a Young Brown Girl*
Barbara Jane Reyes

No. 183 *Mother Country*
Elana Bell

No. 184 *Welcome to Sonnetville, New Jersey*
Craig Morgan Teicher

No. 185 *I Am Not Trying to Hide My Hungers
from the World*
Kendra DeColo

No. 186 *The Naomi Letters*
Rachel Mennies

No. 187 *Tenderness*
Derrick Austin

No. 188 *Ceive*
B.K. Fischer

No. 189 *Diamonds*
Camille Guthrie

No. 190 *A Cluster of Noisy Planets*
Charles Rafferty

No. 191 *Useful Junk*
Erika Meitner

No. 192 *Field Notes from the Flood Zone*
Heather Sellers

Colophon

BOA Editions, Ltd., a not-for-profit publisher of poetry and other literary works, fosters readership and appreciation of contemporary literature. By identifying, cultivating, and publishing both new and established poets and selecting authors of unique literary talent, BOA brings high-quality literature to the public.

Support for this effort comes from the sale of its publications, grant funding, and private donations.

The publication of this book is made possible, in part, by the special support of the following individuals:

Anonymous
Bernadette Catalana
Christopher C. Dahl, *in memory of J. D. McClatchy*
James Long Hale
Anne Havens
Margaret Heminway
Sandi Henschel
Nora A. Jones
Paul LaFerriere & Dorrie Parini
John & Barbara Lovenheim
Joe McElveney
Dan Meyers, *in honor of J. Shepard Skiff*
Boo Poulin
Deborah Ronnen
Sue Stewart, *in memory of Steven L. Raymond*
William Waddell & Linda Rubel
Michael Waters & Mihaela Moscaliuc